SEA TURTLES

BY GAIL GIBBONS

HOLIDAY HOUSE
NEW YORK

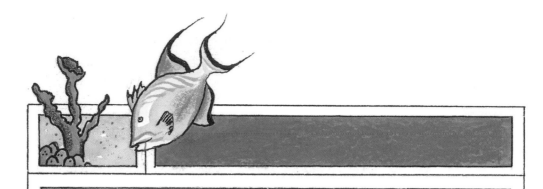

To the Matinicus Island school children

Special thanks to Jerris Foote of Mote
Marine Laboratory, Sarasota, Florida

Copyright © 1995 by Gail Gibbons
All rights reserved
Printed in the United States of America

Library of Congress Cataloging-in-Publication Data
Gibbons, Gail.
    Sea turtles / by Gail Gibbons. — 1st ed.
        p.   cm.
    ISBN 0-8234-1191-5
    1. Sea turtles—Juvenile literature.   [1. Sea turtles.
2. Turtles.]   I. Title.
QL666.C536G525   1995   94-48579   CIP   AC
597.92—dc20

    ISBN 0-8234-1373-X (pbk.)

Sea turtles live in warm ocean waters. They are in the family of air breathing reptiles. Reptiles are cold blooded and have scaly skin.

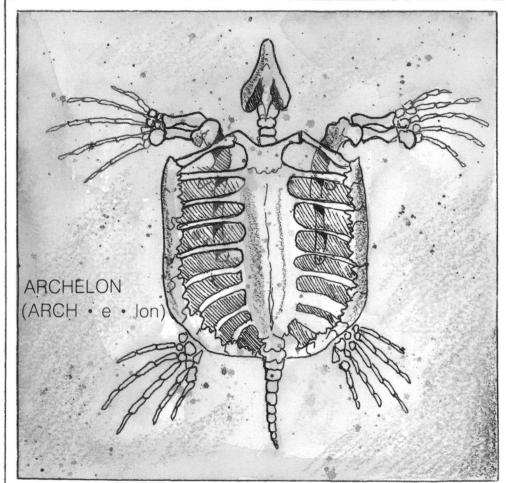

ARCHELON
(ARCH • e • lon)

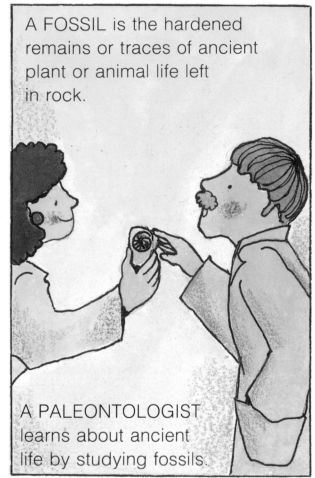

A FOSSIL is the hardened remains or traces of ancient plant or animal life left in rock.

A PALEONTOLOGIST learns about ancient life by studying fossils.

The first sea turtles lived about 200 million years ago. Dinosaurs still roamed earth. Not long ago paleontologists found a fossil skeleton of one of these prehistoric turtles. They named it Archelon. Archelon was so big that if it were still alive today a car could park between its flippers.

Over millions of years sea turtles evolved to become smaller and smaller. Today they are among the oldest surviving creatures in the world.

CARAPACE
(KAR • ah • pace)

SCUTES
(SCOOTS)

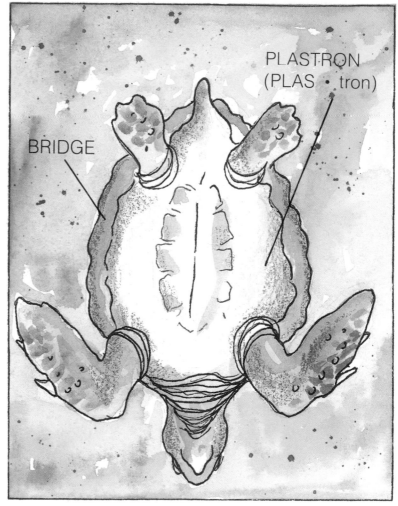

PLASTRON
(PLAS • tron)

BRIDGE

Almost every sea turtle has a shell that is hard and bony for protection. The shell has two parts. The top is called the carapace. The bottom is called the plastron. They are connected by bony bridges. Large scales, called scutes, cover the carapace.

FRONT FLIPPERS

BACK FLIPPERS

A sea turtle has strong flippers it uses like paddles. The front flippers make the sea turtle a powerful swimmer. Some can even swim as fast as 20 miles an hour. That's four times faster than a human can swim. The back flippers are used for turning and stopping.

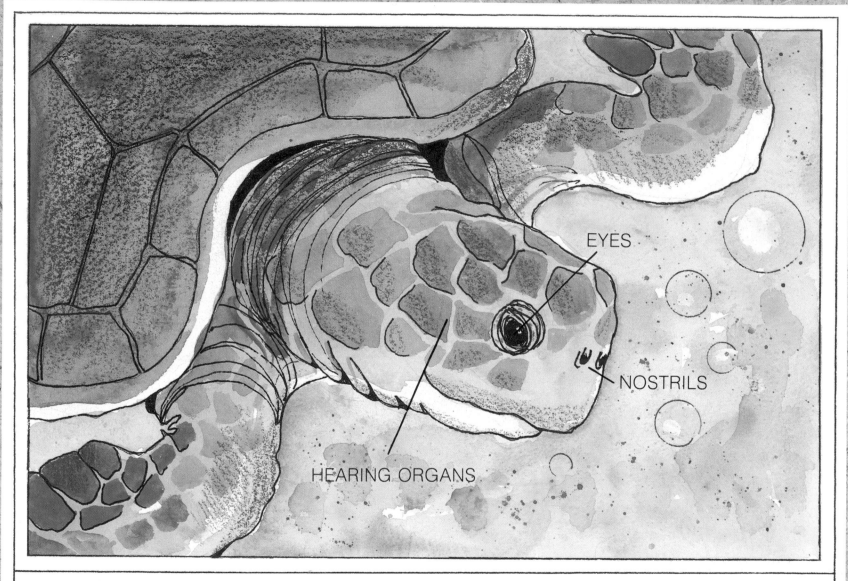

EYES

NOSTRILS

HEARING ORGANS

A sea turtle has sharp senses. It has special hearing organs in the head just behind its eyes. A sea turtle's sense of smell is well developed, too, and it can see far away underwater.

TEAR

Sometimes a sea turtle looks like it's crying but it isn't sad. The tears are how a sea turtle gets rid of some of the sea salt it absorbs from sea water. Most turtles are able to pull their heads, feet and tails inside their shells for protection. Sea turtles can't. Their eyes and ears must always be on the alert.

KEMP'S RIDLEY
SEA TURTLE

OLIVE RIDLEY
SEA TURTLE

There are eight kinds of sea turtles. Seven of them have hard shells. The Kemp's ridley and the olive ridley sea turtles are the smallest. They can be about two feet long and can weigh about 100 pounds. The Kemp's ridley is gray. The olive ridley has more green in its color.

HAWKSBILL
SEA TURTLE

Next in size is the hawksbill sea turtle. About three feet long, it usually weighs about 100 pounds. It is called the hawksbill sea turtle because its upper jaw hooks down and over the lower jaw like a hawk's bill.

AUSTRALIAN FLATBACK
SEA TURTLE

BLACK SEA TURTLE (also called the
EAST PACIFIC GREEN SEA TURTLE)

The Australian flatback sea turtle and the black sea turtle are a little over three feet long. The Australian flatback sea turtle is found in the waters around Australia. The black sea turtle is sometimes called the East Pacific green sea turtle.

The green sea turtle and the loggerhead sea turtle are about the same size. They are usually three to five feet long and weigh about 400 pounds. The green turtle gets its name because of the color of the fat found in its flesh. This is because the green turtle's diet is mainly made up of sea grass. It is the only sea turtle that is a vegetarian. That means it only eats plants.

The loggerhead sea turtle looks a little different than the green turtle. It has a thicker neck and a bigger head. Also the loggerhead has five scutes on each side of its shell instead of four, and two nails on each of its front flippers instead of one.

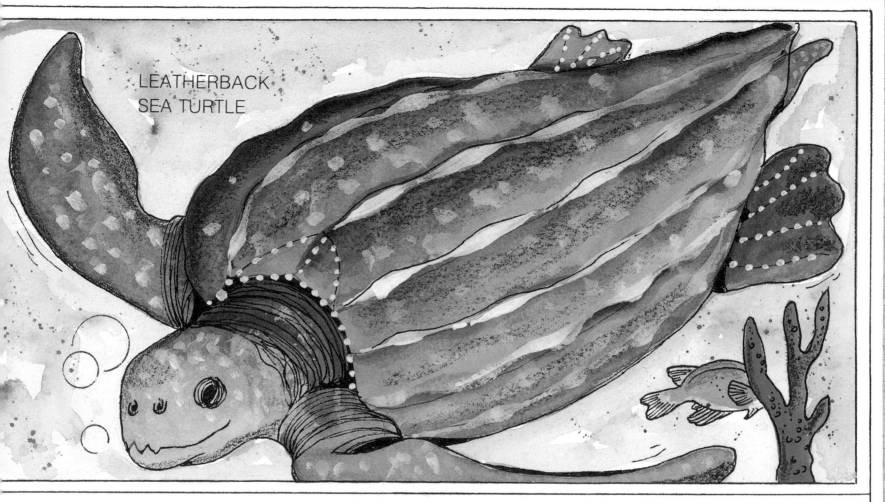

LEATHERBACK
SEA TURTLE

The leatherback is the biggest of all sea turtles. It can be about seven feet long and can weigh over 1000 pounds. It is the only sea turtle without a hard shell. Seven ridges go down its leathery back. The leatherback is the deepest diver of all sea turtles. It can go as deep as 1300 feet.

Sea turtles don't have teeth. They bite and tear their food with their strong jaws. They swallow their food whole. Most sea turtles eat seaweed, fish, crabs and jellyfish. Some sea turtles hiss when they are scared or angry.

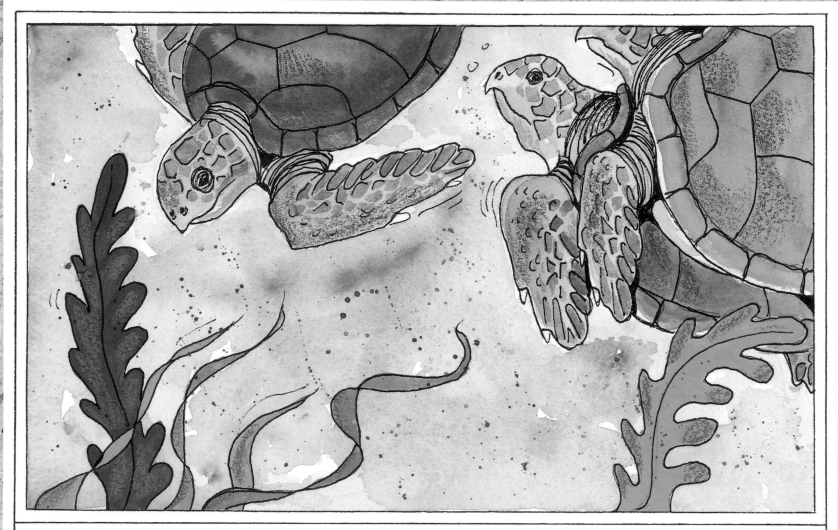

Sea turtles migrate, or travel, to the place where they will have their young. Sometimes they migrate more than 1000 miles to nest. They do this every two to three years in the late spring and summer. They mate in warm seawater.

A few weeks later the female sea turtles return to the same stretch of beach where they were born. It is the only time they will ever leave their ocean home.

It's nesting time. At night the female sea turtle awkwardly drags herself far up onto the beach. She digs a shallow pit to rest in. With her flippers she scoops out a nesting hole. It takes about one hour for her to lay about 100 soft leathery eggs. They look like small white balls. A group of eggs is called a clutch.

She covers them up with sand or dirt. While she is out of the water she is in danger. She can't see well and moves very slowly. Enemies could attack her or her eggs. As fast as she can go, the sea turtle wriggles back to the sea where she will stay until she is ready to make another nest.

 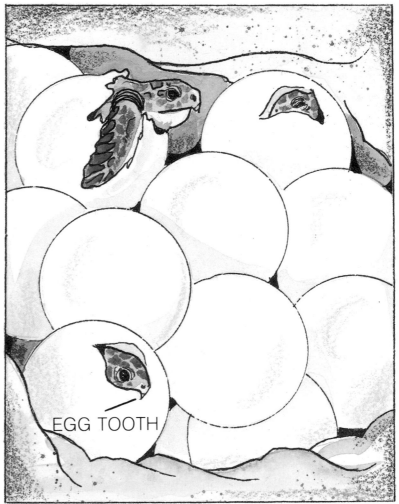

EGG TOOTH

Often the nest eggs are in danger. Sometimes people or animals dig them up for food. In about two months the baby turtles begin to hatch. They use a sharp egg tooth to break their shells open.

Usually during the night they push themselves up through the sand and rush to the sea for protection. Even though it is dark, they know where the sea is. They move away from land toward the sea because the sky appears brighter over it.

PLANKTON

Once at sea they swim with the current and float in beds of seaweed to hide and protect themselves. They eat tiny plants and small animals called plankton. In about two weeks they lose their egg tooth. They migrate to where adult sea turtles live. Life in the sea is dangerous. Whales, sharks and fish often eat them. Only a few turtles survive to be adults but some can live to be over 100 years old.

Today there are fewer sea turtles than ever before. People have hunted them for their meat and their shells, and have dug up turtle eggs for food. Many sea turtle nesting beaches have been destroyed because of people being there.

Some kinds of sea turtles are almost gone forever, or extinct. Today many people want to help them. In many places it is against the law to hunt sea turtles or steal their eggs.

Some organizations have turtle watches. They guard and protect the nesting areas when the females come onshore to nest.

Often sea turtles come to a beach that is developed. In some areas friends of the sea turtles carefully collect the eggs and move them to a safe beach or to a turtle hatchery.

It is good to protect these fascinating creatures and the oceans they live in. Like all other ocean life, sea turtles play an important role in the balance of nature.

Sea turtles remind us of earth's long history. They have been around for millions of years. Scientists and people who care about sea turtles are always learning more about them.

THE DIFFERENCE BETWEEN A SEA TURTLE

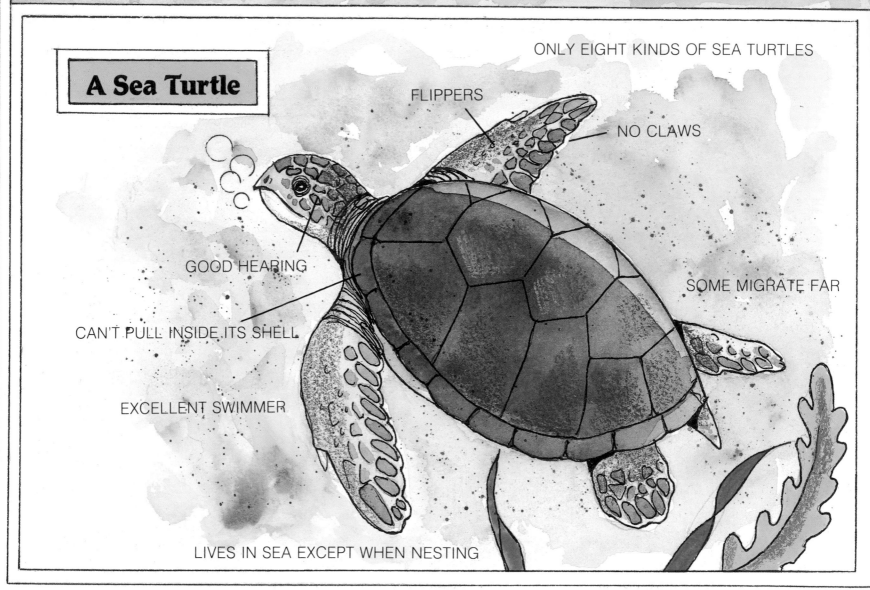

A Sea Turtle

ONLY EIGHT KINDS OF SEA TURTLES

FLIPPERS

NO CLAWS

GOOD HEARING

SOME MIGRATE FAR

CAN'T PULL INSIDE ITS SHELL

EXCELLENT SWIMMER

LIVES IN SEA EXCEPT WHEN NESTING

AND A TURTLE

A Turtle

ABOUT 240 KINDS OF TURTLES

MOST DON'T HEAR WELL

DOESN'T MIGRATE

CAN PULL INSIDE ITS SHELL

WEBBED FEET

CLAWS

SOME ARE GOOD SWIMMERS

LIVES ON LAND AND IN FRESH WATER

...SEA TURTLES...SEA TURTLES...

The ridley sea turtle is the only sea turtle that nests during daylight hours.

The leatherback sea turtle has interlocking pieces of bone, like a jigsaw puzzle, directly under its thick leathery back.

The loggerhead sea turtle may swim 40 miles a day in its search for food.

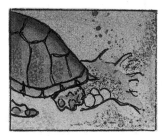

Sea turtles grow slowly. A female loggerhead sea turtle can't lay eggs until she's between 15 and 30 years old.

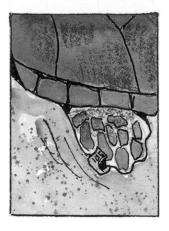

Some scientists tag sea turtles with stainless steel flipper tags to track them. One tagged sea turtle was found in the Azores that had been tagged and released in Brazil, 4000 miles away.

Some scientists estimate the world sea turtle population has dropped in half over the last 20 years.

One year the Mote Marine Laboratory in Florida helped rescue and release more than 146,000 baby sea turtles.